THIS BOOK BELONGS TO:

_____

_____

_____

_____

WEDDING PLANNING TO-DO'S

DATE: _____

WEDDING PLANNING TO-DO'S

DATE: _____

WEDDING PLANNING TO-DO'S

DATE: _____

WEDDING PLANNING TO-DO'S

DATE: _____

WEDDING PLANNING TO-DO'S

DATE: _____

_____

_____

_____

_____

_____

_____

_____

_____

_____

_____

_____

_____

_____

_____

_____

_____

_____

_____

_____

_____

_____

_____

_____

WEDDING PLANNING TO-DO'S

DATE: _____

WEDDING PLANNING TO-DO'S

DATE: _____

_____

_____

_____

_____

_____

_____

_____

_____

_____

_____

_____

_____

_____

_____

_____

_____

_____

_____

_____

_____

_____

_____

_____

_____

WEDDING PLANNING TO-DO'S

DATE: _____

WEDDING PLANNING TO-DO'S

DATE: _____

_____

_____

_____

_____

_____

_____

_____

_____

_____

_____

_____

_____

_____

_____

_____

_____

_____

_____

_____

_____

_____

_____

_____

_____

WEDDING PLANNING TO-DO'S

DATE: _____

WEDDING PLANNING TO-DO'S

DATE: _____

WEDDING PLANNING TO-DO'S

DATE: _____

WEDDING PLANNING TO-DO'S

DATE: _____

_____

_____

_____

_____

_____

_____

_____

_____

_____

_____

_____

_____

_____

_____

_____

_____

_____

_____

_____

_____

_____

_____

_____

_____

WEDDING PLANNING TO-DO'S

DATE: _____

WEDDING PLANNING TO-DO'S

DATE: _____

_____

_____

_____

_____

_____

_____

_____

_____

_____

_____

_____

_____

_____

_____

_____

_____

_____

_____

_____

_____

_____

_____

_____

WEDDING PLANNING TO-DO'S

DATE: _____

WEDDING PLANNING TO-DO'S

DATE: _____

WEDDING PLANNING TO-DO'S

DATE: _____

WEDDING PLANNING TO-DO'S

DATE: _____

WEDDING PLANNING TO-DO'S

DATE: _____

WEDDING PLANNING TO-DO'S

DATE: _____

WEDDING PLANNING TO-DO'S

DATE: _____

WEDDING PLANNING TO-DO'S

DATE: _____

_____
_____
_____
_____
_____
_____
_____
_____
_____
_____
_____
_____
_____
_____
_____
_____
_____
_____
_____
_____
_____
_____
_____

WEDDING PLANNING TO-DO'S

DATE: _____

WEDDING PLANNING TO-DO'S

DATE: _____

_____
_____
_____
_____
_____
_____
_____
_____
_____
_____
_____
_____
_____
_____
_____
_____
_____
_____
_____
_____
_____
_____
_____

WEDDING PLANNING TO-DO'S

DATE: _____

WEDDING PLANNING TO-DO'S

DATE: _____

_____

_____

_____

_____

_____

_____

_____

_____

_____

_____

_____

_____

_____

_____

_____

_____

_____

_____

_____

_____

_____

WEDDING PLANNING TO-DO'S

DATE: _____

WEDDING PLANNING TO-DO'S

DATE: _____

_____

_____

_____

_____

_____

_____

_____

_____

_____

_____

_____

_____

_____

_____

_____

_____

_____

_____

_____

_____

WEDDING PLANNING TO-DO'S

DATE: _____

WEDDING PLANNING TO-DO'S

DATE: _____

WEDDING PLANNING TO-DO'S

DATE: _____

WEDDING PLANNING TO-DO'S

DATE: _____

WEDDING PLANNING TO-DO'S

DATE: _____

WEDDING PLANNING TO-DO'S

DATE: _____

WEDDING PLANNING TO-DO'S

DATE: _____

WEDDING PLANNING TO-DO'S

DATE: _____

_____

_____

_____

_____

_____

_____

_____

_____

_____

_____

_____

_____

_____

_____

_____

_____

_____

_____

_____

_____

_____

WEDDING PLANNING TO-DO'S

DATE: _____

WEDDING PLANNING TO-DO'S

DATE: _____

WEDDING PLANNING TO-DO'S

DATE: _____

WEDDING PLANNING TO-DO'S

DATE: _____

WEDDING PLANNING TO-DO'S

DATE: _____

WEDDING PLANNING TO-DO'S

DATE: _____

_____

_____

_____

_____

_____

_____

_____

_____

_____

_____

_____

_____

_____

_____

_____

_____

_____

_____

_____

_____

_____

_____

_____

_____

_____

_____

WEDDING PLANNING TO-DO'S

DATE: _____

WEDDING PLANNING TO-DO'S

DATE: _____

WEDDING PLANNING TO-DO'S

DATE: _____

WEDDING PLANNING TO-DO'S

DATE: _____

_____
_____
_____
_____
_____
_____
_____
_____
_____
_____
_____
_____
_____
_____
_____
_____
_____
_____
_____
_____
_____
_____
_____
_____
_____

WEDDING PLANNING TO-DO'S

DATE: _____

WEDDING PLANNING TO-DO'S

DATE: _____

_____

_____

_____

_____

_____

_____

_____

_____

_____

_____

_____

_____

_____

_____

_____

_____

_____

_____

_____

_____

_____

WEDDING PLANNING TO-DO'S

DATE: _____

WEDDING PLANNING TO-DO'S

DATE: _____

_____

_____

_____

_____

_____

_____

_____

_____

_____

_____

_____

_____

_____

_____

_____

_____

_____

_____

_____

_____

_____

_____

_____

_____

WEDDING PLANNING TO-DO'S

DATE: _____

WEDDING PLANNING TO-DO'S

DATE: _____

WEDDING PLANNING TO-DO'S

DATE: _____

WEDDING PLANNING TO-DO'S

DATE: _____

WEDDING PLANNING TO-DO'S

DATE: _____

WEDDING PLANNING TO-DO'S

DATE: _____

WEDDING PLANNING TO-DO'S

DATE: _____

WEDDING PLANNING TO-DO'S

DATE: _____

_____

_____

_____

_____

_____

_____

_____

_____

_____

_____

_____

_____

_____

_____

_____

_____

_____

_____

_____

_____

_____

_____

_____

_____

WEDDING PLANNING TO-DO'S

DATE: _____

WEDDING PLANNING TO-DO'S

DATE: _____

WEDDING PLANNING TO-DO'S

DATE: _____

WEDDING PLANNING TO-DO'S

DATE: _____

WEDDING PLANNING TO-DO'S

DATE: _____

WEDDING PLANNING TO-DO'S

DATE: _____

WEDDING PLANNING TO-DO'S

DATE: _____

WEDDING PLANNING TO-DO'S

DATE: _____

WEDDING PLANNING TO-DO'S

DATE: _____

WEDDING PLANNING TO-DO'S

DATE: _____

WEDDING PLANNING TO-DO'S

DATE: _____

WEDDING PLANNING TO-DO'S

DATE: _____

WEDDING PLANNING TO-DO'S

DATE: _____

WEDDING PLANNING TO-DO'S

DATE: _____

WEDDING PLANNING TO-DO'S

DATE: _____

WEDDING PLANNING TO-DO'S

DATE: _____

WEDDING PLANNING TO-DO'S

DATE: _____

WEDDING PLANNING TO-DO'S

DATE: _____

WEDDING PLANNING TO-DO'S

DATE: _____

WEDDING PLANNING TO-DO'S

DATE: _____

WEDDING PLANNING TO-DO'S

DATE: _____

WEDDING PLANNING TO-DO'S

DATE: _____

_____
_____
_____
_____
_____
_____
_____
_____
_____
_____
_____
_____
_____
_____
_____
_____
_____
_____
_____
_____
_____
_____
_____
_____
_____
_____
_____
_____

WEDDING PLANNING TO-DO'S

DATE: _____

WEDDING PLANNING TO-DO'S

DATE: _____

WEDDING PLANNING TO-DO'S

DATE: _____

WEDDING PLANNING TO-DO'S

DATE: _____

WEDDING PLANNING TO-DO'S

DATE: _____

WEDDING PLANNING TO-DO'S

DATE: _____

_____
_____
_____
_____
_____
_____
_____
_____
_____
_____
_____
_____
_____
_____
_____
_____
_____
_____
_____
_____
_____
_____
_____
_____
_____
_____
_____

WEDDING PLANNING TO-DO'S

DATE: _____

WEDDING PLANNING TO-DO'S

DATE: _____

_____
_____
_____
_____
_____
_____
_____
_____
_____
_____
_____
_____
_____
_____
_____
_____
_____
_____
_____
_____
_____
_____
_____
_____
_____

WEDDING PLANNING TO-DO'S

DATE: _____

WEDDING PLANNING TO-DO'S

DATE: _____

_____
_____
_____
_____
_____
_____
_____
_____
_____
_____
_____
_____
_____
_____
_____
_____
_____
_____
_____
_____
_____
_____
_____
_____
_____
_____
_____

WEDDING PLANNING TO-DO'S

DATE: _____

WEDDING PLANNING TO-DO'S

DATE: _____

WEDDING PLANNING TO-DO'S

DATE: _____

WEDDING PLANNING TO-DO'S

DATE: _____

WEDDING PLANNING TO-DO'S

DATE: _____

WEDDING PLANNING TO-DO'S

DATE: _____

WEDDING PLANNING TO-DO'S

DATE: _____

WEDDING PLANNING TO-DO'S

DATE: _____

_____

_____

_____

_____

_____

_____

_____

_____

_____

_____

_____

_____

_____

_____

_____

_____

_____

_____

_____

_____

_____

_____

_____

_____

WEDDING PLANNING TO-DO'S

DATE: _____

WEDDING PLANNING TO-DO'S

DATE: _____

WEDDING PLANNING TO-DO'S

DATE: _____

WEDDING PLANNING TO-DO'S

DATE: _____

WEDDING PLANNING TO-DO'S

DATE: _____

WEDDING PLANNING TO-DO'S

DATE: _____

_____

_____

_____

_____

_____

_____

_____

_____

_____

_____

_____

_____

_____

_____

_____

_____

_____

_____

_____

_____

_____

_____

_____

WEDDING PLANNING TO-DO'S

DATE: _____

WEDDING PLANNING TO-DO'S

DATE: _____

Made in the USA
Lexington, KY
01 September 2017